The Best Sport

Cameron Macintosh

The Best Sport

Text: Cameron Macintosh
Publishers: Tania Mazzeo and Eliza Webb
Series consultant: Amanda Sutera
Hands on Heads Consulting
Editor: Kirstie Innes-Will
Project editor: Annabel Smith
Designer: Leigh Ashforth
Project designer: Danielle Maccarone
Permissions researcher: Lumina Datamatics
Production controller: Renee Tome

Acknowledgements
We would like to thank the following for permission to reproduce copyright material:

Front cover, pp, 4 (top), 6 (top), 30 (top): Lopolo/Shutterstock.com; back cover, p. 1: Auncha/Adobe Stock Photos; p. 4 (bottom): SAEED KHAN/AFP/Getty Images; p. 5: sot/Photodisc/Getty Images; p. 6 (bottom): Zamrznuti tonovi/Shutterstock.com; p. 7: Dmytro Zinkevych/Shutterstock.com; p. 8 (top): Alex Slitz/Getty Images Sport/Getty Images, (bottom): Kelly Defina/Getty Images Sport/Getty Images; p. 9 (top): poltu shyamal/Shutterstock.com, (bottom): Adrian Sherratt/Alamy Stock Photo; p. 10: WESTOCK PRODUCTIONS/Shutterstock.com; p. 11 (top): Cameron Spencer/Getty Images Sport/Getty Images, (bottom): Mark Evans/Getty Images Sport/Getty Images; p. 12 (top): New Africa/Shutterstock.com, (bottom): Olena Afanasova/Alamy Stock Photo; p. 13: Alex Bogatyrev/Shutterstock.com; p. 14 (top): dpa picture alliance/Alamy Stock Photo, (bottom): "Pressefoto Baumann /SIPA USA"; p. 15 (top): iStock.com/Phynart Studio, (bottom): lechatnoir/E+/Getty Images; p. 16: iStock.com/E+/CasarsaGuru; p. 17 (top): Independent Photo Agency/Alamy Stock Photo, (bottom): ANNE-CHRISTINE POUJOULAT/AFP/Getty Images; p. 18 (top): NICOLAS TUCAT/AFP/Getty Images, (bottom): ROBYN BECK/AFP/Getty Images; p. 19: MediaNews Group/Orange County Register via Getty Images/MediaNews Group/Getty Images; p. 20 (top): ZUMA Press, Inc./Alamy Stock Photo, (bottom): ROBYN BECK/AFP/Getty Images; p. 21 (top): photosindia/photosindia/Getty Images, (bottom): iStock.com/Dsafanda; p. 22: MichaelSvoboda/E+/Getty Images; p. 23 (top): Stephen Dunn/Getty Images Sport/Getty Images, (bottom): Sean M. Haffey/Getty Images; p. 24 (top): Bruce Laurance/Tetra images/Getty Images, (bottom): Kris Timken/Tetra images/Getty Images; p. 25: PeopleImages/iStock/Getty Images; p. 26 (top): Matt Roberts - FIFA/FIFA/Getty Images, (bottom): Cameron Spencer/Getty Images Sport/Getty Images; p. 27 (top): SolStock/E+/Getty Images, (bottom): sot/Photodisc/Getty Images; p. 28: PA Images/Alamy Stock Photo; p. 29 (top): Mackenzie Sweetnam/Getty Images Sport/Getty Images, (bottom): Ben Hoskins/Getty Images Sport/Getty Images; p. 30 (bottom): bikeriderlondon/Shutterstock.com.

NovaStar

ISBN 978 0 17 033482 2

Cengage Learning Australia
Level 5, 80 Dorcas Street
Southbank VIC 3006 Australia
Phone: 1300 790 853
Email: aust.nelsonprimary@cengage.com

For learning solutions, visit **cengage.com.au**

Printed in China by 1010 Printing International Ltd
1 2 3 4 5 6 7 29 28 27 26 25

Nelson acknowledges the Traditional Owners and Custodians of the lands of all First Nations Peoples. We pay respect to Elders past and present, and extend that respect to all First Nations Peoples today.

Contents

Which Sport Is the Best?

Hi, I'm Tristan! My friends and I are going to tell you about our favourite sports, and why each of us thinks our sport is the best. We'll also tell you about some of the famous athletes who play these sports and inspire us.

Different sports appeal to different people, for all sorts of reasons. For example, some people prefer to compete on their own, so they choose individual sports such as surfing and skateboarding. People who enjoy teamwork can choose team sports such as soccer, basketball or cricket.

Soccer is very popular with children of all ages.

As some of my friends will point out, certain sports are particularly good for people with different abilities or disabilities. For example, the rules of tennis can be **adapted** so that it can be played by people who use wheelchairs.

With so many great options, it's no wonder that my friends and I feel strongly about our favourite sports!

In wheelchair tennis, the ball is allowed to bounce twice before it is hit back over the net.

Basketball

My favourite sport is basketball, and here's why!

First, I like basketball because it's a team sport. There are usually five players on each side. To do well in our games, my teammates and I need to work closely together. For example, if one of us is nearer to the hoop than the others, we pass the ball to them to increase our chances of scoring. This kind of cooperation brings us closer together as a team and as friends.

In basketball, you score points by shooting the ball through the hoop.

Second, basketball is a high-energy sport, which is perfect if you have as much energy as I do! I'm exhausted by the end of a game, but I feel great – especially if my team wins!

Furthermore, basketball has helped me develop all sorts of skills. One of the most important skills in basketball is passing, which is when one player throws or bounces the ball to another. An equally important skill is shooting, which is when a player throws the ball up to the hoop in the hope of scoring.

Last of all, basketball has helped me to run faster and become more **agile**. This is important because basketball players need to dart around the court at high speed and change direction quickly, depending on where the ball goes. These skills are useful when I play other sports, too, such as soccer and volleyball.

For all these reasons, basketball is absolutely the greatest sport there is!

Basketball players need to be fit and agile.

Patty MILLS

A player who inspired me to take up basketball is Patty Mills. Patty plays for the Australian men's team – the Boomers – and has played for several high-profile teams in the USA. He was also the captain of the Australian men's team at the 2020 Olympics, where they won a bronze medal. Patty is super skilled at shooting three-pointers, which is when a player shoots a basket far from the hoop. This is a skill I'm working on, too!

Patty Mills has played for several US teams, including the Atlanta Hawks.

Cricket

Hi, I'm Brianna, and my biggest **passion** is cricket!

One great thing about cricket is that every player on a team can contribute in many ways. For example, everyone gets to field, which is when players spread out around the cricket oval and collect or catch the ball after the batter hits it. Some players get to bat, too. Batters score by hitting the ball and running between the **wickets**, or by hitting it to the **boundary** of the oval. I'm a bowler, which means that I contribute by bowling, or throwing, the ball to the batters, and trying to get them out by hitting the wickets with the ball.

Batters try to hit the ball as far as possible.

Another great thing about cricket is that there's a form of the game to suit everyone. For example, Test matches, which are played by adult cricketers, last for up to five days. I like watching Test matches. So much can change from day to day – sometimes one team seems to be winning but the next day the other team is on top. There are also shorter forms of cricket, in which each team only bats for a limited time. These matches are usually over in two or three hours. They are perfect for kids, and for adults who can't spend five days playing a match!

Yet another fantastic thing about cricket is that so many people know how to play it because it's popular around the world, particularly in countries such as the United Kingdom, India, New Zealand and Australia.

Cricket is an amazing sport that can be played anywhere. Some of the best games I've played have been with friends in my backyard. All you need is a bat, a ball and a friend or two!

It is easy to set up a game of cricket with friends.

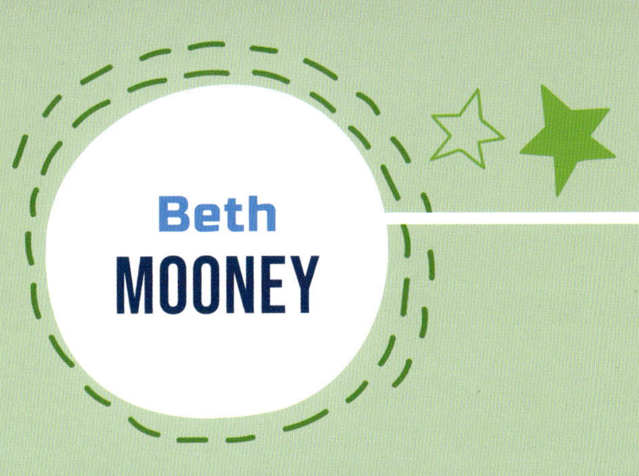

Beth MOONEY

My biggest hero is an Australian cricketer called Beth Mooney. Beth has played for the Australian women's team since 2016 and is particularly good at batting. This led to her being named Leading Woman Cricketer in the World for 2020 and 2022. Beth was successful from a young age – she was chosen to play for the Queensland team in 2010, just after she turned 16!

Beth was the world's number one batter in women's Twenty20 International cricket in 2020.

Dance Sports

Hi! I'm Caleb, and I'm **passionate** about dance sports. Dance sports are a range of dance **styles** that can be performed competitively as a **solo** dancer, **duo** or group.

One reason I like dance sports so much is that they are very athletic.

Many dance moves require a lot of strength and **flexibility**. Dancing takes a lot of **stamina**, too. I do a lot of practising and competitions. Because of this, I've become very fit.

The second great thing about dance sport is that it's so **versatile**. There are a range of different types of dance. The dance sport I participate in is **Latin dancing**, but there are other categories of dance sports, including traditional ballroom dancing and breaking (also called breakdancing). Each dance style has different types of music, too.

Latin dancing is often fast and energetic.

Traditional ballroom dancing is performed as a duo.

Furthermore, dance sports are a really great way to make friends. When I dance with a partner or in a group, we have to support each other so that we dance as well as we possibly can. The trust we build with each other as we practise and compete can make our friendships very strong.

If you like music and enjoy high-energy movement, I'm sure you'll agree with me that dance sports are the greatest!

Marius-Andrei BALAN

One of the dancers I admire most is Marius-Andrei Balan. Marius-Andrei was born in Romania but now lives in Germany. He started dancing at the age of seven. Marius-Andrei is particularly good at Latin dancing and has won many competitions, including the European and World championships. He often dances as a duo with his wife, Kristina Moshenska.

Marius and Kristina are one of the most successful dance sport duos in the world.

Judo

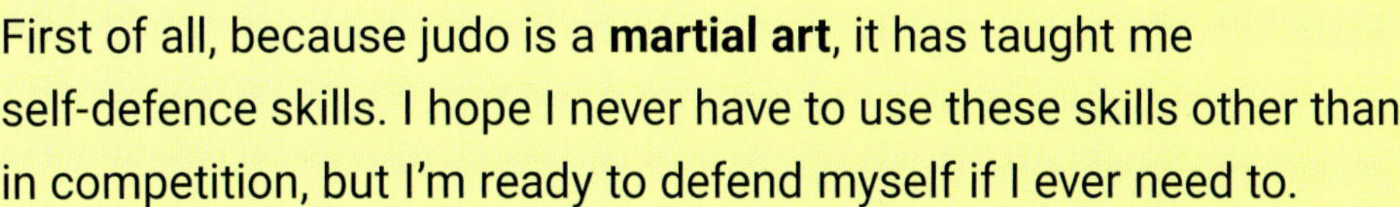

Hi, I'm Tilly, and I don't think there's any better sport than judo!

First of all, because judo is a **martial art**, it has taught me self-defence skills. I hope I never have to use these skills other than in competition, but I'm ready to defend myself if I ever need to.

Second, judo teaches me about Japan and its **culture**. Judo was invented in Japan, so we use Japanese words. For example, the word "judo" means "gentle way", because in judo we don't hit or kick our opponents. Instead, we throw our opponents and try to pin them down.
A person who learns or competes in judo is a *judoka*. The place where we learn and practise judo is called a *dojo*.

Judokas learn how to throw their opponents to the ground.

Third, I get to compete in **tournaments**. I learn a lot by testing my skills against other kids of my level. We begin each match with a bow. **Respect** for our opponent is an essential part of judo, and it makes our tournaments extra special. Everyone feels that their skills are valued.

Opponents bow to each other to show respect before competing in a judo tournament.

Lastly, judo gives me clear goals to work towards. We're rewarded for our progress with different coloured belts. In Australia, we start on a white belt. We can then progress to yellow, orange, green, blue, brown and black belts. I'm currently a green belt. It's an awesome feeling when our coach awards us our next belt.

I hope I've convinced you that judo really is the best sport!

Teddy RINER

My favourite judoka is Teddy Riner, from France. He's the first judoka to have won 11 gold medals at the World Judo Championships, which are held in a different country each year. Teddy won his medals between 2007 and 2017. He's 2.04 metres tall – almost the height of a door in a house. No wonder people call him Big Ted!

Teddy Riner lost only nine times in international competitions.

Adaptive Surfing

Hi, I'm Cally. I absolutely love adaptive surfing, also called "para surfing", and think it's by far the best sport! Adaptive surfing is a form of surfing for people with disabilities.

The best thing about adaptive surfing is that people with various disabilities can enjoy it. I only have about 8 per cent vision, but I can still enjoy the waves and develop my surfing skills. Adaptive surfing is an ideal sport for me because I use my **sense** of touch to feel how the water is moving, which helps me surf in harmony with it. I can also hear the waves coming behind me and prepare myself to ride them. I love the feeling of freedom as I ride down a wave.

In adaptive surfing, people with many different disabilities can enjoy the thrill of riding waves.

An instructor teaches a young adaptive surfer to ride a wave.

Another fantastic thing about adaptive surfing is that you can compete in tournaments, with categories for people with different disabilities. There are categories for people who are **visually impaired**, like me.

Furthermore, through adaptive surfing I've developed many great friendships at my adaptive surfing club. We help each other get better at riding the waves, and at swimming, each time we go out in the water. We're supporting each other and keeping safe, too.

Adaptive surfing is incredibly fun and exciting. If you have any kind of disability or vision impairment – or even if you don't – I'm sure you'll agree with me that it's the best sport ever!

Matt FORMSTON

One of my heroes is Matt Formston. Matt is blind – he has lost nearly all his vision. As he got older, he became increasingly determined not to let this stop him from competing as an athlete. Matt started as a **para-cyclist** and then switched to adaptive surfing. He has now won three World Championships as an adaptive surfer and works hard to encourage vision-impaired kids like me to try surfing.

Matt Formston has a passion for surfing.

Skateboarding

Hi, I'm Hassan, and I'm here to tell you that skateboarding is the coolest sport there is!

First, I love skateboarding because there are so many awesome tricks you can learn. One of the first tricks I learnt is called the "manual". This is when I ride my board just on its two back wheels. I do this by putting more of my weight on the back of the board so that the front of it goes up. Some other tricks I'm practising right now are the "kickflip" and the "power slide". The more tricks I learn, the more fun skateboarding becomes.

Skateboarders develop very good balance.

Second, you can skateboard almost anywhere you can find an even surface – indoors or outdoors. Ramps are awesome places to skate and learn tricks, too. You can skateboard just for fun by yourself or with friends.

Third, if you want, you can also skate in competitions. In my latest competition, each skater was given 45 seconds to impress the judges. The judges scored us on how well we performed our tricks, and how our tricks flowed together. Skating in competitions motivates me to keep practising and getting better and better.

Skateboarding is the best sport. You really have to give it a try!

Skateboarders learn lots of different tricks.

Alexis SABLONE

One of the skateboarders I admire most is Alexis Sablone. As a child, Alexis learnt to skateboard by watching videos of others and copying their moves. She has competed in many competitions, including the World Skateboarding Championships. Alexis also competed at the Tokyo Olympics in 2020, the first Olympic Games to include skateboarding as a sport.

Alexis Sablone has been competing in skateboarding competitions since she was 12.

Soccer

Hi, I'm Sanjay, and I think soccer is the world's best sport!

One reason soccer's a great game is that it takes a lot of skill and fitness to play well. Most players in a soccer match can only use their feet or heads to touch the ball, so they need to be particularly skilled at controlling the ball with just their feet.

Furthermore, soccer is one of the few sports that has a goalkeeper who guards the net – and that's my position! I'm the only player in my team who's allowed to touch the ball with their hands, to stop it going into the net or to throw it to teammates. This makes it even more fun for me, although I'm under a lot of pressure to stop the other team from scoring!

The goalkeeper can catch the ball to stop it going into the net.

Winning a soccer match is a great feeling.

Last of all, I love the fact that soccer is one of the most popular sports played around the world. It's often referred to as "the world game", because it's played in so many countries. Every four years, the world comes together to watch the FIFA World Cup. It's an incredibly exciting time.

Soccer is an awesome game that requires lots of great skills. It really is the world's best sport!

Mackenzie ARNOLD

One of my favourite soccer players is Mackenzie Arnold, the goalkeeper for the Australian women's soccer team, the Matildas. Mackenzie first played for the Matildas in 2012, at the age of 18. Eleven years later, she was so successful at stopping goals in the 2023 Women's World Cup that she became known as Australia's "brick wall"!

Mackenzie Arnold helped Australia's women's soccer team reach fourth place in the 2023 FIFA World Cup.

Wheelchair Tennis

Hi! My name's Tasmin, and I'm here to tell you why wheelchair tennis is the best sport.

The thing I like most about wheelchair tennis is that it gives many people with disabilities the chance to enjoy playing tennis. As a person who uses a wheelchair to get around, it's the perfect sport for me. Some of the rules between regular tennis and wheelchair tennis are different, which demonstrates how tennis can be adapted. For example, in regular tennis, the ball can only bounce once before the player hits it back over the net with their racquet. In wheelchair tennis it can bounce twice. This gives players in wheelchairs more time to get to the ball to hit it back.

In wheelchair tennis, special tennis wheelchairs are used to get around the court quickly.

In addition, wheelchair tennis can be played by one player against another (singles) or by two players against another two players (doubles). Some of the most enjoyable times I've had on the court have been when I've played doubles alongside my friend Ella.

Lastly, wheelchair tennis helps me stay fit and strong, especially my arms and upper body. This is because I use my arms to move my wheelchair around, as well as to hit the ball with my racquet.

Wheelchair tennis is incredibly fun to play, and amazing to watch, too! No other sport comes close!

Playing doubles wheelchair tennis with a partner can create great friendships.

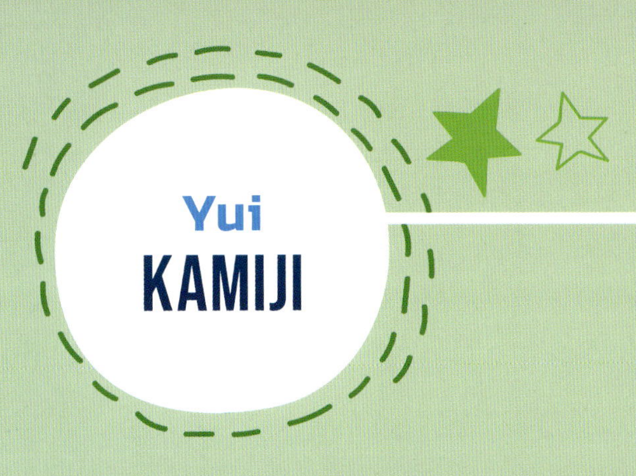

Yui KAMIJI

My favourite wheelchair tennis player is Yui Kamiji from Japan. Yui has won many tournaments around the world, as well as Paralympic medals as both a singles and doubles player at the 2020 Paralympics in Tokyo. Yui started playing wheelchair tennis at the age of 11 – only one year older than I am now!

Yui Kamiji has won 28 major tennis tournaments.

Passion and Purpose

Although we all have different reasons for loving a particular sport, I can see why my friends are so passionate about their own favourite sports. Each has a range of features and qualities that makes it special.

Patty Mills once said: "Basketball as a sport has brought me happiness, joy, education and a real sense of purpose." This makes me think that whichever sport you like best, the most important thing is simply joining in and enjoying all the incredible experiences it can give you.

Friendships made through sport can last a lifetime.

Glossary

adapted (*adjective*)	changed in particular ways, for a particular reason
agile (*adjective*)	able to move about quickly
boundary (*noun*)	the edge of the playing field in cricket
culture (*noun*)	the way a particular group of people lives and expresses itself
duo (*noun*)	two people working together
flexibility (*noun*)	the ability to bend or stretch easily
Latin dancing (*noun*)	dance styles that were developed in Latin America, a group of countries in Central and South America
martial art (*noun*)	a set of fighting and self-defence skills
passion (*noun*)	very strong enthusiasm for something
para-cyclist (*noun*)	a cyclist with a disability
passionate (*adjective*)	being very enthusiastic about something
respect (*noun*)	polite feelings shown towards a person
sense (*noun*)	one of the ways we receive information from our environment – sight, hearing, taste, touch or smell
solo (*adjective*)	done by one person alone
stamina (*noun*)	the ability to keep doing something for a long time
styles (*noun*)	the particular ways something is done
tournaments (*noun*)	sporting competitions in which competitors compete for a prize over several rounds
versatile (*adjective*)	able to be used many different ways
visually impaired (*adjective*)	partially or completely blind
wickets (*noun*)	the sets of three wooden poles (stumps) at either end of a cricket pitch

Index